pinpoint ENGLISH
whole class reading

Flexible and Creative Lessons for

Chasing the Sun

Stories from Africa
edited by Véronique Tadjo

Y6

Published by Pearson Education Limited, 80 Strand, London, WC2R 0RL.

www.pearsonschools.co.uk

Text © Pearson Education Limited 2019
Edited by Pearson Education Limited and Just Content Limited
Designed and typeset by Pearson Education Limited and PDQ Media
Original illustrations © Pearson Education Limited 2019
Illustrated by PDQ Media
Characters illustrated by The Boy Fitz Hammond
Cover design by Pearson Education Limited 2019
Cover illustration © Pearson Education Limited 2019

The right of Sarah Loader to be identified as author of this work has been asserted by her in accordance with the Copyright, Designs and Patents Act 1988.

First published 2019

22 21 20 19
10 9 8 7 6 5 4 3 2 1

British Library Cataloguing in Publication Data
A catalogue record for this book is available from the British Library

ISBN 978 1 292 27404 1

Copyright notice
All rights reserved. The material in this publication is copyright. Activity sheets may be freely photocopied for classroom use in the purchasing institution. However, this material is copyright and under no circumstances may copies be offered for sale. If you wish to use the material in any way other than that specified you must apply in writing to the publishers.

Printed in the UK by Ashford Press Ltd

Note from the publisher
Pearson has robust editorial processes, including answer and fact checks, to ensure the accuracy of the content in this publication, and every effort is made to ensure this publication is free of errors. We are, however, only human, and occasionally errors do occur. Pearson is not liable for any misunderstandings that arise as a result of errors in this publication, but it is our priority to ensure that the content is accurate. If you spot an error, please do contact us at resourcescorrections@pearson.com so we can make sure it is corrected.

Contents

Programme overview	4
Using Whole Class Reading	5
Activity planning guide	6
Synopsis	8
Starter activities	9
Main activities	21
Plenary activities	36
Photocopiable masters	53
Answers	64

Programme overview

Introduction

Pinpoint English Whole Class Reading is your new go-to resource for flexible, high-quality activities based on the best children's books, with a strong focus on turning readers into writers and developing rich vocabularies.

Whole Class Reading is curriculum-matched, allowing you to target the skills required to ensure success in the national curriculum for English.

Principles

- As the teacher, you can choose which texts to teach in which order, matching with your focus topic for a particular week or term, the needs of your class or just your personal favourites.
- Each text has been chosen by an experienced panel of children's writers, librarians and teachers.
- The Whole Class Reading series allows you to rediscover classroom favourites as well as explore new titles that champion diversity and broaden your class's horizons.
- Activities provide opportunities to engage with fiction, poetry and non-fiction, with curriculum objectives provided for each task.
- Reading comprehension is taught through discussion and written activities, providing practice of essential skills.
- Spoken language skills are improved through lively debate, discussions and games.
- Vocabulary, spelling and grammar are taught in the context of a real writer's choices.
- Activities are differentiated where appropriate yet complementary so that the whole class can enjoy reading together.

Programme structure

- Whole Class Reading provides a vast, flexible range of starter, main and plenary activities to empower you to teach with confidence.
- Review the activities, pinpoint the skills you want to cover and build engaging lessons.
- Look out for differentiated activities to allow you to keep the whole class together.

 These tasks provide a low-threshold starting point to build the foundations of understanding.

 These tasks are pitched at age-related expectations so that children who can complete the work confidently and accurately display a firm grasp of the topic or skill.

 These tasks challenge children to explore the topic or skill in greater depth.

Using Whole Class Reading

Suggested **activity timings** are shown here. Some activities can be carried out over several lessons.

Resource lists let you know which photocopy masters and materials you will need.

Milestones suggest how far you should read before carrying out the activity.

Vocabulary builder activities help children to expand their vocabularies.

Vocabulary quiz

4 x 20 Vocabulary builder **Resources required**: photocopy masters (PCM) 4–7

DURING READING

- **Children should be able to:**
  use relevant strategies to build their vocabulary.

1 At four points during reading, explain that the class is going to play a quiz, using vocabulary from the stories. It can be played as a class or in pairs.

2 Photocopy the following.
   - PCM 4 (for quiz 1 after pages 9–24)
   - PCM 5 (for quiz 2 after pages 61–71)
   - PCM 6 (for quiz 3 after pages 101–113)
   - PCM 7 (for quiz 4 after pages 115–121)

3 As you read each question, children need to work out the word that is described.

   T Write the answers, or first letters of them, on the board in a random order, so that children just have to match the correct word to the definition.

Plenary activities 5–8

Each activity explores areas of the **national curriculum**.

The main activity steps are pitched at the 'Securing' level. Where appropriate, you will find **differentiation ideas** here.

Curriculum areas covered in this title

- spoken language
- reading
- spelling, punctuation and grammar
- writing
- music
- design and technology
- science
- geography
- art and design

Activity planning guide

The magic of Whole Class Reading is that you can mix and match activities in a way that works for you, your class and the time you can dedicate to *Chasing the Sun*. Sometimes, you might spend a whole lesson reading; at other times, you might build a structured lesson from the 90 activities you'll find in this book. Below is an overview of these activities, complete with reading milestones (in brackets) and pairing suggestions.

Starter activities

1: *Speaking* (after *Introduction*)
Consider the evolution of African literature.

2: *Writing* (before *Sun, Wind and Cloud*)
Think about weather types.

3: *Drama* (after *Sun, Wind and Cloud*)
Role play interviews with a character from the story.

4: *Drama* (after *The Drum*)
Role play interviews with a character from the story.

5: *Drama* (after *A Lion Hunt*)
Role play interviews with a character from the story.

6: *Drama* (after *Sosu's Call*)
Role play interviews with a character from the story.

7: *Drama* (after *The Little Blue Boy*)
Role play interviews with a character from the story.

8: *Drama* (after *Sun, Win and Cloud*)
Role play interviews with a character from the story.

9: *Reading* (after *Why the Mosquito Lives in the Bush*)
Order events from the story.

10: *Speaking* (after *The Drum*)
Debate whether Tortoise was right or wrong.

11–12: *Speaking* (after *A Lion Hunt*)
Think about important moments in our lives over two sessions.

13: *Drama* (after *Leuk-the-Hare Discovers Man*)
Create freeze frames.

14: *Drama* (after *Sosu's Call*)
Create freeze frames.

Main activities

1: *Reading; geography* (before reading)
Write quizzes about Africa.
Use the quizzes in Plenary 1.

2: *Writing* (after *Sun, Wind and Cloud*)
Write a sequel, introducing Snow.

3–4: *Science* (after *Sun, Wind and Cloud*)
Conduct an experiment to find the most powerful weather.
This is a two-lesson mini-project.

5: *Writing* (after *Leuk-the-Hare Discovers Man*)
Write a memoir.

6–7: *Speaking* (after *Why the Mosquito Lives in the Bush*)
Hold a trial to find out who was responsible for the owl's death.
This is a two-lesson mini-project and works well with Main 8.

8: *Writing* (after *Why the Mosquito Lives in the Bush*)
Write the mosquito's plea.
Works well with Mains 6–7.

9: *Writing* (after *The Drum*)
Write a sequel to The Drum.

10: *Speaking* (after *The Drum*)
Decide on a suitable punishment for Tortoise.

11: *Writing* (after *The Drum*)
Write an entry in Tortoise's diary.

12: *Writing* (after *A Lion Hunt*)
Write an entry in the narrator's diary.

13: *Writing* (after *Sosu's Call*)
Write an entry in Sosu's diary.

14: *Writing* (after *The Little Blue Boy*)
Write an entry in the boy's diary.

15: *Writing* (after *Citronella*)
Write an entry in Citronella's diary.

Plenary activities

1: *Geography* (before reading)
Answer an Africa quiz.
Use the quizzes from Main 1.

2: *Vocabulary* (before *Sun, Wind and Cloud*)
Match the adjectives to the characters.

3: *Drama* (before *Leuk-the-Hare Discovers Man*)
Freeze-frame moments from the story.

4: *Writing; speaking* (after *Leuk-the-Hare Discovers Man*)
Imagine Leuk's revenge.

5: *Vocabulary* (after *Leuk-the-Hare Discovers Man*)
Find the vocabulary in the story.

6: *Vocabulary* (after *A Lion Hunt*)
Find the vocabulary in the story.

7: *Vocabulary* (after *Bulubulu and Bamboko*)
Find the vocabulary in the story.

8: *Vocabulary* (after *Miss Johnson*)
Find the vocabulary in the story.

9: *Speaking* (after *Why the Mosquito Lives in the Bush*)
Invent an alternative version of events.

10: *Vocabulary* (before *The Drum*)
Discover new words.

11: *Vocabulary* (before *A Lion Hunt*)
Discover new words.

12: *Music* (after *Sosu's Call*)
Compose a piece of drum music.

13: *Art* (after reading *Half a Day*)
Create an artist's impression of either the before or after scene.

Starter activities

15: *Writing* (after *The Little Blue Boy*)
Consider our similarities and differences.

16: *Reading* (after *Half a Day*)
Think about cause and effect in the real world.

17: *Speaking* (after *Half a Day*)
Think about how the world has changed.

18: *Writing* (after *Half a Day*)
Write eye-catching headlines.
Works well before Mains 16–18.

19: *Writing* (before *Bulubulu and Bamboko*)
Create a rat fact file.
Works well with Plenary 15.

20: *Speaking* (after *Miss Johnson*)
Talk about a life-changing event.

21: *Speaking* (before *Citronella*)
Listen to our pulses.

22: *Reading* (during *A Lion Hunt*)
Picture the scene.

23: *Reading* (during *Citronella*)
Picture the scene.

24: *Vocabulary* (after *Citronella*)
Create new onomatopoeic words.
Works well before Mains 27–30.

25: *Writing* (after *Citronella*)
Write a piece of flash fiction focusing on one of the senses.

26: *Reading* (after reading)
Think about the stories' messages.
Works well with Main 25.

27: *Speaking* (after reading)
Choose a favourite story.

28: *Drama* (after reading)
Play charades with the story titles.

29: *Speaking* (after reading)
Order the animals from least to most powerful.
Complete before Starter 30.

30: *Speaking* (after reading)
Play a game of African animal showdown.
Play this game after Starter 29.

Main activities

16–18: *Writing* (after *The Little Blue Boy*)
Write a newspaper article about the birth of Little Blue Boy.
This is a three-lesson mini-project and works well with Starter 18.

19–20: *Writing* (after *Bulubulu and Bamboko*)
Create travel documentaries about Lagos, Nigeria.
This is a two-lesson mini-project.

21: *Design; art* (after *Bulubulu and Bamboko*)
Design a dream house.

22: *Writing* (after *Miss Johnson*)
Write about a day in our lives.

23: *Writing* (after *Citronella*)
Write a story about life without one of the senses.

24: *Art* (after *Father, Who Are You?*)
Draw a portrait or make a model of someone important.

25: *Writing* (after reading)
Write a story with a message.
Works well with Starter 26.

26: *Writing* (after reading)
Write an animal fable.

27: *Writing* (after reading)
Write a poem inspired by Leuk-the-Hare.

28: *Writing* (after reading)
Write a poem inspired by Iguana.

29: *Writing* (after reading)
Write a poem inspired by Tortoise.

30: *Writing* (after reading)
Write a poem inspired by the rat.

Plenary activities

14: *Writing; art* (after *Half a Day*)
Draw or write about how the world has changed.

15: *Art; science* (before *Bulubulu and Bamboko*)
Create a rat habitat.
Works well after Starter 19.

16: *Writing* (after *Bulubulu and Bamboko*)
Compare the story's rat habitats.

17: *Reading* (after *Bulubulu and Bamboko*)
Predict what happens next.

18: *Speaking* (after *Miss Johnson*)
Discuss what Miss Johnson might do next.

19: *Vocabulary; grammar* (after *Miss Johnson*)
Find antonyms in the story.
Works well before Plenary 20.

20: *Vocabulary* (after *Miss Johnson*)
Describe things we like and dislike.
Works well after Plenary 19.

21–22: *Music* (after *Citronella*)
Create powerful soundscapes over two sessions.

23: *Reading* (after *Father, Who Are You?*)
Order the emotions experienced by Boniswa.

24: *Music* (after reading)
Choose a musical theme for each story.

25: *Speaking* (after reading)
Pitch one of the stories to a TV company.

26–27: *Drama* (after reading)
Learn and recite poetry by heart over two sessions.

28: *Geography* (after reading)
Locate African countries on a map.

29: *Geography; writing* (after reading)
Create a country fact file.

30: *Geography; writing* (after reading)
Compare two countries.

Synopsis

Chasing the Sun

This is a collection of 12 stories from across Africa, which brings together traditional folklore and contemporary tales. They give insight into the literary background of a continent, and also the historical context that frames it.

The collection starts with stories inspired by the oral tradition of storytelling. By the middle of the collection, the style has changed, with stories written more for the engagement of young people today – stories about coming of age, growing up and understanding the complexities of life. Towards the end of the book, the stories change again, covering first the disillusionment related to independence and freedom from colonisation, and then finally, at the very end, hope for the future.

Within this wide contextual range, the stories offer huge variety in terms of tone and style, with drama *(A Lion Hunt* and *Sosu's Call)*, humour *(Why the Mosquito Lives in the Bush, Bulubulu and Bamboko)*, and poignancy *(Half a Day, Citronella* and *Father, Who Are You?)*. There is an assortment of topics, characters and plots, providing something for every type of reader and, when read back-to-back, there is a real sense of travelling through a changing world.

About the authors

The authors – Chinua Achebe, Meshack Asare, Kariuki Gakuo, P Gurrey, Fatou Keïta, Joseph Lemasolai Lekuton, Naguib Mahfouz, Naiwu Osahon, Karen Press, Léopold Sédar Senghor, Carl de Souza and Véronique Tadjo – come from across Africa, covering literary tradition and historical context from Ghana, Côte d'Ivoire, Kenya, Egypt, Nigeria, South Africa, Senegal and Mauritius.

The editor – Véronique Tadjo – was born in Paris but grew up in Côte d'Ivoire. She has written novels and several collections of poems. She is also an illustrator, and provided the illustrations for this collection. She has a BA in English and a doctorate in African American Literature and Civilisation.

Starter activities

Literature through time

**AFTER READING
INTRODUCTION**

- **Children should be able to:**

   use spoken language to develop understanding through speculating, hypothesising, imagining and exploring ideas; participate in discussions, presentations, performances, role play, improvisations and debates.

   increase their familiarity with a wide range of books, including books from other cultures and traditions.

1. Once you've read the book's introduction, display the following themes of African literature on the board. Write them in this order, but without the numbers in brackets (which show the correct order).
   - Coming of age (2)
   - Oral traditional style (1)
   - Reflections of hope (5)
   - Reflections of independence and democracy (4)
   - Impact of colonial powers (3)

2. Ask the class to put the different stages in the correct order to form a timeline of themes in African literature.

   D Children could research and write briefly about how the different themes in literature reflect the continent's historical background.

— Starter activity 1

Sun, Wind and Cloud

**BEFORE READING
SUN, WIND
AND CLOUD**

- **Children should be able to:**

   articulate and justify answers, arguments and opinions; participate in discussions; listen and respond appropriately to adults and their peers; consider and evaluate different viewpoints, attending to and building on the contributions of others.

   note and develop initial ideas, drawing on reading and research where necessary.

1. Divide the class into pairs or groups of three and ask children to write a pros and cons list of the different weather types (sun, wind, clouds).

2. Explain that the groups should have a separate list for every weather type, but should then draw some conclusions and briefly explain which weather they think is the most useful and which is the most dangerous or negative.

   T Children could tackle one weather type each in their group.

— Starter activity 2

Role play

DURING READING

6 × ⏱15

- **Children should be able to:**

 ask relevant questions to extend their understanding and knowledge; give well-structured descriptions, explanations and narratives for different purposes, including for expressing feelings; maintain attention and participate actively in collaborative conversations; participate in discussions, presentations, performances, role play, improvisations and debates.

 draw inferences such as inferring characters' feelings, thoughts and motives from their actions, and justify inferences with evidence.

1. After you have read each story below, divide the class into pairs and explain that one person in each pair should role-play an interviewer, and the other a character from that story.

2. Interviewers should think about some good questions that will delve into the personality of the character. Remind children to ask mainly open questions, using stems such as 'how…' or 'why…'.

3. Children in role as a character should focus on portraying the character's personality accurately. They should think about how that character feels during the events of the story, and how their feelings might change. Remind them to include evidence from the text in their answers.

4. Give the interviewers between five and ten minutes to interview their partners.
   - *Sun, Wind and Cloud* (p 17): an interview with the Sun, Wind or Cloud
   - *The Drum* (p 59): an interview with the tortoise
   - *A Lion Hunt* (p 71): an interview with the narrator
   - *Sosu's Call* (p 82): an interview with Sosu
   - *The Little Blue Boy* (p 92): an interview with the blue boy
   - *Father, Who Are You?* (p 137): an interview with Boniswa

5. Once interviews have concluded, children come back together and interviewers explain their findings.

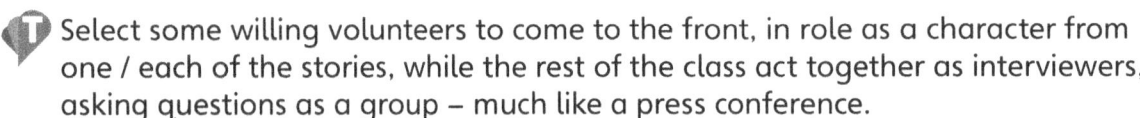 Select some willing volunteers to come to the front, in role as a character from one / each of the stories, while the rest of the class act together as interviewers, asking questions as a group – much like a press conference.

Ensure that all children get the opportunity to play both a character and an interviewer.

Starter activities 3–8

Sequence of events

AFTER READING
WHY THE MOSQUITO LIVES IN THE BUSH

 Resources required: photocopy master (PCM) I

- **Children should be able to:**

   listen and respond appropriately to adults and their peers; articulate and justify answers, arguments and opinions; consider and evaluate different viewpoints, attending to and building on the contributions of others.

  summarise the main ideas drawn from more than one paragraph, identifying key details that support the main ideas; explain and discuss their understanding of what they have read.

1 Divide the class into groups of four and hand out PCM I. Ask each group to number the events in the order in which they happen in *Why the Mosquito Lives in the Bush*.

2 Explore children's answers together, correcting and clarifying as necessary.

You could extend this activity by asking children to turn over their worksheets and draw a timeline, illustrating it with animal drawings.

Starter activity 9

Debate

AFTER READING
THE DRUM

- **Children should be able to:**

   articulate and justify answers, arguments and opinions; maintain attention and participate actively in collaborative conversations; participate in discussions, presentations, performances, role play, improvisations and debates; consider and evaluate different viewpoints, attending to and building on the contributions of others.

   explain and discuss their understanding of what they have read.

1 Once you have read *The Drum*, explain that children are going to have a debate to discuss whether Tortoise's actions were right or wrong.

2 Divide the class into two groups, explaining that one group will be defending Tortoise, and the other will be arguing against him.

3 Encourage all members of both sides to participate. If prompts or starting points are needed, ask the following questions.

- What does Tortoise do that is positive for his fellow creatures?
- Does it matter if Tortoise is greedy and dishonest if he provides food for so many?
- What damage does Tortoise ultimately do?
- Who does Tortoise harm?
- Is Tortoise fit to be king?

Starter activity 10

All about me

AFTER READING
A LION HUNT

2 x

- **Children should be able to:**

  listen and respond appropriately to adults and their peers; ask relevant questions to extend their understanding and knowledge; give well-structured descriptions, explanations and narratives for different purposes, including for expressing feelings; maintain attention and participate actively in collaborative conversations.

1 Once you've read *A Lion Hunt*, discuss how the narrator made a decision that had a big impact on his life and how afterwards he longed for an opportunity to prove that he wasn't a coward.

2 Divide the class into pairs, one child will be the interviewer and the other the interviewee. In each session, ask the interviewers to think of some questions to ask, and the interviewees to prepare their answers. Give children between five and ten minutes to interview each other.

3 **In the first session,** children interview each other about an important moment of self-realisation in their lives, when they learnt something about themselves. For example, perhaps they discovered that they were better at something than they thought, or more scared / braver than expected in a situation.

4 **In the second session,** children interview each other about a moment of bravery in their lives. This doesn't have to be physically brave; it can be overcoming any sort of fear or challenge or just doing something outside of their comfort zone.

5 Ask each pair to come to the front and explain to the rest of the class what they learnt about each other.

Starter activities 11–12

Freeze frame

DURING READING

2 x

- **Children should be able to:**

  participate in discussions, presentations, performances, role play, improvisations and debates; articulate and justify answers, arguments and opinions; give well-structured descriptions, explanations and narratives for different purposes, including for expressing feelings.

1 Divide the class into groups of three or four.

2 Explain that children are going to choose a scene from the stories below that has particular significance for them and create a freeze frame of it.
   - **Session 1:** Ask each group to choose a scene from *Leuk-the-Hare Discovers Man*.
   - **Session 2:** Ask each group to choose a scene from *Sosu's Call*.

3 Ask each group to perform their still scene at the front of the class.

4 The class then needs to try to guess the scene that each group has created.

5 Once the scene has been guessed correctly, ask children to explain why they chose it, what it means to them and why it is particularly significant.

Starter activities 13–14

Similarities and differences

**AFTER READING
THE LITTLE
BLUE BOY**

- **Children should be able to:**

 use further organisational and presentational devices to structure text and to guide the reader; select appropriate grammar and vocabulary.

 listen and respond appropriately to adults and their peers; ask relevant questions to extend their understanding and knowledge; maintain attention and participate actively in collaborative conversations.

1 Divide the class into pairs. Each pair is going to create a list of what is similar and different between the two of them. Encourage children to think beyond their physical appearance to where they live, who's in their family, what their cultural background is, what their likes and dislikes are, etc.

2 Ask some pairs to feed back to the class. Can children add any similarities or differences that the pairs have missed?

Starter activity 15

While I was at school

**AFTER READING
HALF A DAY**

- **Children should be able to:**

 articulate and justify answers, arguments and opinions; give well-structured descriptions, explanations and narratives for different purposes; use spoken language to develop understanding through speculating, hypothesising, imagining and exploring ideas; participate in discussions, presentations, performances, role play, improvisations and debates.

 explain and discuss their understanding of what they have read.

1 Once you've read *Half a Day*, divide the class into groups of three or four and ask children to think about all the things that change during the narrator's half day at school.

- The streets have an influx of vehicles.
- Many more people fill the streets.
- High buildings replace gardens and fields.
- Rubbish is piled up on the streets.

2 Each group considers which of the changes would have the biggest impact on the narrator and presents a case for why it would have such a big effect. Encourage children to think specifically about cause and effect.

If there are strong differences of opinion, set up a debate to encourage children to coherently argue their point of view.

Starter activity 16

Changing world

AFTER READING
HALF A DAY

- **Children should be able to:**

listen and respond appropriately to adults and their peers; articulate and justify answers, arguments and opinions; consider and evaluate different viewpoints, attending to and building on the contributions of others; maintain attention and participate actively in collaborative conversations.

1 Ask children to think about things that have changed in the world since they started school.

2 Encourage as many contributions as possible, such as environmental, technological, scientific. They could be global (the hole in the ozone layer shrinking) or local (a new park / housing development).

3 Ask children to talk about the impact of these changes on them, their community and the wider world.

This activity could be extended into a main activity such as a debate, or children could work on an awareness campaign or a 'ways to help' initiative.

Starter activity 17

Hot topic

AFTER READING
HALF A DAY

Resources required: headlines on global topics from various newspapers

- **Children should be able to:**

identify the audience for and purpose of the writing; select appropriate grammar and vocabulary; use further organisational and presentational devices to structure text and to guide the reader.

1 Cut out and display headlines on different global topics from a variety of newspapers.

2 Children are going to think about some potential news stories from the future and write newspaper headlines and taglines for them.

3 Children can work individually, in pairs or small groups and the stories can be anything of global interest – either connected to current events or completely imagined, e.g. the discovery of life on other planets, the extinction of specific species, the destruction of parts of the natural world, dramatic changes in the school system.

4 Encourage children to think of gripping, eye-catching headlines, how much information they want to give in the tagline, and what their angle is.

You could provide a number of scenarios for children to choose from, either from the examples above, or your own.

This activity works well with Main activities 16–18.

Starter activity 18

Rat fact file

**BEFORE READING
BULUBULU AND BAMBOKO**

 Resources required: access to the internet, books about rats, paper, coloured pencils

- **Children should be able to:**

 identify the audience for and purpose of the writing; select appropriate grammar and vocabulary; use further organisational and presentational devices to structure text and to guide the reader; assess the effectiveness of their own and others' writing.

 retrieve, record and present information from non-fiction.

1 Before reading *Bulubulu and Bamboko*, explain to the class that it's a story about rats.

2 Divide the class into groups of two or three and explain that they're going to research and collect information about rats and create a rat fact file.

3 Children's rat fact files should include some basic information about rats: size, weight, different species, life expectancy, habitats, diet, etc.

4 Remind children to use a variety of devices to structure the text and make it easier for the reader, e.g. bullet points, labels or captions. Ask children to include a picture in their fact file, either drawn or sourced online.

5 Once the fact files are finished, encourage children to swap them with each other and feed back on anything new that they have learnt or something useful that is missing.

This activity works well with Plenary activity 15.

Starter activity 19

It changed my life

**AFTER READING
MISS JOHNSON**

- **Children should be able to:**

 listen and respond appropriately to adults and their peers; ask relevant questions to extend their understanding and knowledge; give well-structured descriptions, explanations and narratives for different purposes, including for expressing feelings; maintain attention and participate actively in collaborative conversations.

1 Divide the class into pairs and explain that they're going to discuss a significant moment in their lives that changed them. This can be something that's happened to their family (moving, divorce, new siblings, a loss), something that's happened to them personally (starting a new school, joining a club, an event or holiday) or something that's happened in the community or world around them.

2 Give children five to ten minutes to share their experiences with each other.

3 If there's time, and depending on the sensitivity of the experiences, you could invite pairs to come up and share their partners' experiences with the class.

Starter activity 20

Feel the pulse

  Resources required: stopwatches

**BEFORE READING
CITRONELLA**

 • **Children should be able to:**

listen and respond appropriately to adults and their peers; participate in discussions, presentations, performances, role play, improvisations and debates.

 listen with attention to detail and recall sounds.

1. Before reading *Citronella*, explain that children are going to listen to each other's pulses.
2. Divide the class into pairs and ask children to jump up and down for one minute to increase their pulse rate. Children then take it in turns to place their fingers on the neck or inside wrist of their partner in order to feel their pulse.
3. Encourage children to time it for one minute before swapping over.
4. Invite children to tap out the pulse on the table and feed back to the wider group what the sound of their partner's pulse reminded them of.

Starter activity 21

Imagination activity

DURING READING

 2 x

 • **Children should be able to:**

give well-structured descriptions, explanations and narratives for different purposes, including for expressing feelings; participate in discussions, presentations, performances, role play, improvisations and debates.

 draw inferences such as inferring characters' feelings, thoughts and motives from their actions, and justify inferences with evidence.

1. Explain that this is an imagination activity to bring two of the stories to life.
2. Ask children to listen, eyes closed, picturing the scene that you read aloud.
3. Encourage children to use all of their senses to imagine what it would look, sound, smell and taste like and how it would feel.
   - *A Lion Hunt:* Read aloud page 64 (the lion attack), including the sentence that continues onto page 65.
   - *Citronella:* Read aloud page 125 (Citronella and Grandpa-Tambalakok's journey to the beach) to the final sentence above the image on page 127.
4. Once you've finished reading, gather feedback on how it felt to 'be there'.

   Children could select an evocative scene from one of the stories and read it aloud to the rest of the class, a small group or a partner to bring it to life.

Starter activities 22–23

Onomatopoeia

 Vocabulary builder

**AFTER READING
CITRONELLA**

- **Children should be able to:**
  > listen and respond appropriately to adults and their peers; maintain attention and participate actively in collaborative conversations; give well-structured descriptions, explanations and narratives for different purposes, including for expressing feelings.

1 Explain that children are going to write some onomatopoeic words that imitate the thing they're describing, e.g. trickled-tickled, fffff-leee, togodok.

2 Encourage children to think about their walk to and from school, different types of weather, the school environment, etc., to come up with ideas.

3 Gather feedback from as many children as possible and consider displaying the examples around the classroom.

T Narrate the experience of walking to school so that children can jump in with onomatopoeic sounds for the actions that you describe.

D Children could try writing some short poems using their onomatopoeic words.

These words could be used for further activities such as Main activities 27–30.

Starter activity 24

The senses

**AFTER READING
CITRONELLA**

- **Children should be able to:**
  > identify the audience for and purpose of the writing; select appropriate grammar and vocabulary.

  > listen and respond appropriately to adults and their peers; maintain attention and participate actively in collaborative conversations.

1 Explain to children that you're going to do a quick writing exercise to develop one of the senses.

2 Children need to write a short piece (around 350 words) of flash fiction, which focuses specifically on one of the senses, e.g. smell, sound, taste, look or the way something feels.

3 Once children have finished, encourage volunteers to read out their pieces, and ask the rest of the class to feed back on how these pieces made them feel and whether they gave them a new understanding of the sense.

Starter activity 25

Story messages

AFTER READING

- **Children should be able to:**
  summarise the main ideas drawn from more than one paragraph, identifying key details that support the main ideas; explain and discuss their understanding of what they have read; identify and discuss themes and conventions in and across a wide range of writing.

1. Divide the class into pairs and explain that each pair needs to think of the message or moral behind every story in the book and write a subtitle that succinctly explains the author's intended message.

2. Once the pairs have finished these, a game could be played, where the rest of the class has to match the subtitle to its title. The first pair to guess correctly wins a point.

This activity works well with Main activity 25.

Starter activity 26

Book review

AFTER READING

- **Children should be able to:**
  give well-structured descriptions, explanations and narratives for different purposes; participate in discussions, presentations, performances, role play, improvisations and debates; articulate and justify answers, arguments and opinions.

1. Ask some children to describe their favourite story from the book to the rest of the class, and explain why they have chosen it. This can be done as formally or informally as you like.

2. Encourage children to think about what they like about the story, justifying why they've chosen it and what it means to them.

D Children should try to express how their favourite story makes them feel, and be aware that it doesn't have to make them feel good – it can be powerful and significant in other ways, e.g. making them feel sad, moved or disgusted.

This activity could be extended and turned into a main writing activity, with the book reviews displayed around the classroom.

Starter activity 27

Charades

AFTER READING

 Resources required: a plastic bowl

- **Children should be able to:**

  participate in discussions, presentations, performances, role play, improvisations and debates.

1 Write down the story titles from the book on separate pieces of paper, fold them up and put them all in a bowl.

2 Divide the class into groups of three or four and explain that you're going to play a quick game of charades, acting out stories from the book.

3 Each group will assign roles and then mime actions to the rest of the class to help them guess the story.

4 Ask the groups to come to the front of the class one by one and pull a story out of the bowl.

Children could have some practice time to work on their 'act'.

This activity could be adapted to cover different presentation styles, e.g. acting with words (rather than miming), singing, rapping or dancing.

Starter activity 28

African animals

AFTER READING

 Resources required: photocopy master (PCM) 2, scissors, information books or access to the internet

- **Children should be able to:**

  participate in discussions, presentations, performances, role play, improvisations and debates; articulate and justify answers, arguments and opinions; consider and evaluate different viewpoints, attending to and building on the contributions of others.

1 Give each child a copy of PCM 2. Ask them to cut out the animal cards.

2 Explain that these animals are all mentioned in the book and that children may need to do a bit of research to learn more about them.

3 Children rate the animals from 1 to 10, depending on how powerful they think the animals are (1 = the least powerful, 10 = the most powerful). They need to discuss and agree these ratings as a class. It's important that each child allocates the same number to each animal.

You will need to keep hold of the completed cards for Starter activity 30.

Starter activity 29

African animal showdown

AFTER READING

 Resources required: animal cards from Starter activity 29

- **Children should be able to:**

 listen and respond appropriately to adults and their peers; maintain attention and participate actively in collaborative conversations, staying on topic and initiating and responding to comments.

1 Using the numbered cards from Starter activity 29, play a game of *African animal showdown!*

2 Divide the class into groups of four and ensure that every child in each group has a set of the numbered animal cards.

3 Explain the rules of the game:
- Each child in the group gets a set of ten animal cards. They shuffle them and lay them out, face up, in two rows of five.
- Children take 30 seconds to memorise the position of the ten animals and then turn their cards face down.
- The child with the most recent birthday goes first, turning over a card of their choice and placing it in the middle of the table.
- Play moves clockwise around the table, with each child choosing and placing a card.
- Whoever places the most powerful animal (the one with the score closest to 10) wins the 'showdown' and takes all the cards in the pile, placing the pile beside them on the table.
- The winner then goes first in the next round.
- Children need to think tactically, because if very powerful animals have already been placed, it might be better to use a less powerful animal and save the more powerful ones for rounds with a better chance of winning.
- The aim is to have the most animal cards at the end.
- If children place the same animal in the middle, they take their next cards and simultaneously place them in the middle (like in snap), so no tactics can be used.

This game could be played frequently as a starter or plenary.

Starter activity 30

Main activities

True or false — BEFORE READING

 Resources required: information books or access to the internet

- **Children should be able to:**
  - retrieve, record and present information from non-fiction.
  - describe and understand key aspects of physical geography and human geography.

1 Explain that children will write their own true or false quizzes about Africa.

2 In pairs, children will need to research the continent to find out interesting facts – things that might be new to their peers. False statements should be plausible.

3 Each pair should come up with 20 statements on history, geography, culture and nature. Children should also include true / false tick boxes.

You can use children's quizzes in Plenary activity 1.

Main activity 1

Snow sequel — AFTER READING SUN, WIND AND CLOUD

- **Children should be able to:**
  - identify the audience for and purpose of the writing; select appropriate grammar and vocabulary; in narratives, describe settings, characters and atmosphere and integrate dialogue to convey character and advance the action.
  - link ideas across paragraphs using a wider range of cohesive devices.
  - draw inferences such as inferring characters' feelings, thoughts and motives from their actions, and justify inferences with evidence; predict what might happen from details stated and implied.

1 Explain that children are going to write a sequel to *Sun, Wind and Cloud* in which Snow is also a character demonstrating its strength. Children's stories can be short, but should follow a similar structure to the original story and have a title.

2 Encourage children to think about what sort of power Snow might have, how the landscape in a snowy climate might be different, what advantages and disadvantages Snow might have over Sun, Wind and Cloud, and ultimately who would be most powerful. Children should try to use the same style, tone and characters as in the original story, but to give Snow a personality of their own creation: arrogant, humble, bitter, kind, soft, gentle, unfriendly, etc.

 Children could could create a storyboard to tell their story.

 Children should focus on the way that all the characters feel.

Main activity 2

21

Weather conditions experiment

AFTER READING SUN, WIND AND CLOUD

1 x ⏱20 1 x ⏱45 **Resources required:** materials for experiment, as decided by class

- **Children should be able to:**

  - plan different types of scientific enquiries to answer questions, including recognising and controlling variables where necessary; report and present findings from enquiries.

  - use spoken language to develop understanding through speculating, hypothesising, imagining and exploring ideas; participate in discussions, presentations, performances, role play, improvisations and debates.

  - select appropriate grammar and vocabulary; use further organisational and presentational devices to structure text and to guide the reader.

1. Explain that children are going to create an experiment to test which weather condition – heat or water – is the most powerful or damaging.

2. **In the first session,** ask the class to come up with a resource that can be tested, e.g. grass, leaves, paper (all children need to test the same material).

3. Once the resource has been agreed, explain that children need to divide their resource equally. Half is placed under direct heat like a lamp, and the other half is placed in water.

4. Encourage children to check on their experiment at regular time intervals, e.g. every hour, and to make notes on how it's going and what changes they can see.

5. **In the second session,** divide the class into small groups, or pairs, to write up the results of their experiment. They should think about how to present the results as well as explain what the findings mean: how this might have an effect on a broader scale. Ask them to include labelled diagrams.

6. Encourage groups to present their results to the rest of the class, and to explain whether they found anything surprising or interesting.

Main activities 3–4

Memoir

AFTER READING
LEUK-THE-HARE DISCOVERS MAN

- **Children should be able to:**

 identify the audience for and purpose of the writing; select appropriate grammar and vocabulary; use a wide range of devices to build cohesion within and across paragraphs; in narratives, describe settings, characters and atmosphere and integrate dialogue to convey character and advance the action.

 link ideas across paragraphs using a wider range of cohesive devices.

1 Discuss the experience of being new to something, e.g. a new group or new school – how it felt not to know anyone, and how children overcame it.

2 Explain that children will be writing a memoir (a memory of an event) from the perspective of a newcomer. Their memoirs could tell the stories of characters who are new to a town, school, country, family, etc.

3 The memoirs should draw on children's experiences of being new to something, but children can use an imagined character and situation. Remind children that their memoirs should be written in the first person.

T Children should focus on using paragraphs and basic punctuation, such as capital letters, full stops, question marks, commas for lists and apostrophes.

S Children should focus on integrating some dialogue to express character and advance the narration.

D Children should focus on the tone and formality of their memoir, noting the difference in register between writing a memoir and writing a diary.

Main activity 5

Debate the case

2 × 50

> AFTER READING
> **WHY THE MOSQUITO LIVES IN THE BUSH**

- **Children should be able to:**

  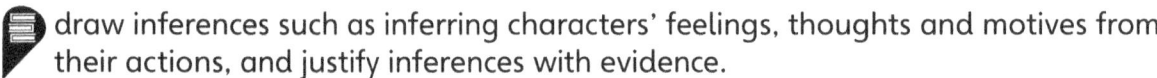 draw inferences such as inferring characters' feelings, thoughts and motives from their actions, and justify inferences with evidence.

  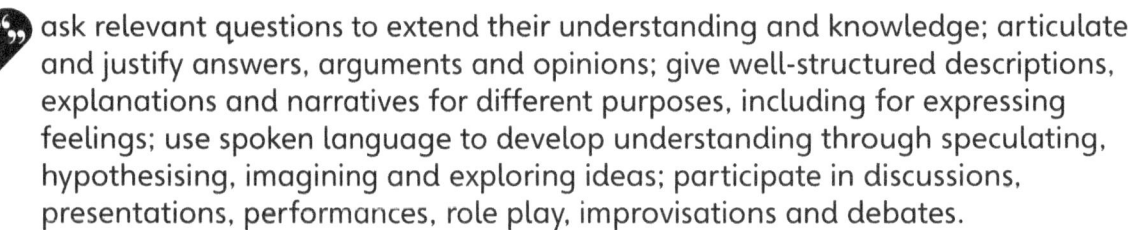 ask relevant questions to extend their understanding and knowledge; articulate and justify answers, arguments and opinions; give well-structured descriptions, explanations and narratives for different purposes, including for expressing feelings; use spoken language to develop understanding through speculating, hypothesising, imagining and exploring ideas; participate in discussions, presentations, performances, role play, improvisations and debates.

1. Explain that you're going to set up a trial to find out who was responsible for the death of the baby owl.

2. Set up a prosecution and defence for the Mosquito by creating two groups of four: one to argue that it was all Mosquito's fault, the other to present a case in Mosquito's defence.

3. Designate roles for the Mosquito and key witnesses, such as the Iguana, Boa constrictor, Rabbit, Crow, Monkey, Owl and Wind. The rest of the class will be the jury. Their role will be to decide whether or not the Mosquito is guilty, based on the evidence.

4. **In the first session,** explain that the prosecution and defence teams need to work out their arguments, making notes about what they want to say, who they will call as witnesses and what they hope to make the jury believe.

5. The witnesses should all work independently to write a short statement about what happened from their perspective, how they played a part and whether they take responsibility or not.

6. The jury need to work together to summarise the story so that it's fresh in their minds for the trial. This can be done orally, through a storyboard or by making notes.

7. **In the second session,** the trial begins. Encourage the class to make this as formal as possible (you could provide some dressing-up clothes), and to think about the order of the trial, e.g. whether the prosecution or defence will go first, how long each team will have to make their case. Remind both prosecution and defence teams that they need to sum up their argument at the end.

8. Once the arguments have been made, the jury needs to make a decision about whether the Mosquito is guilty. When a unanimous verdict has been agreed, they should present this to the 'court'.

T Children go into role as the jury.

S Children go into role as the characters from the story (Mosquito, Iguana, Boa constrictor, Rabbit, Crow, Monkey, Owl and Wind) and aim to ensure that they're consistent and believable in that role.

D Children form the prosecution and defence teams, and aim to put forward a compelling argument, backed up with evidence to support their argument.

Main activities 6–7

Mosquito's plea

AFTER READING
WHY THE MOSQUITO LIVES IN THE BUSH

- **Children should be able to:**

  identify the audience for and purpose of the writing; select appropriate grammar and vocabulary; use a wide range of devices to build cohesion within and across paragraphs; use further organisational and presentational devices to structure text and to guide the reader; assess the effectiveness of their own and others' writing.

  link ideas across paragraphs using a wider range of cohesive devices; use the semi-colon, colon and dash; understand the difference between vocabulary typical of informal speech and vocabulary appropriate for formal speech and writing.

  draw inferences such as inferring characters' feelings, thoughts and motives from their actions, and justify inferences with evidence.

  participate in discussions, presentations, performances, role play, improvisations and debates.

1 Explain to the class that they're going to write a plea in role as the Mosquito. Children need to think about whether the Mosquito will take responsibility for his actions or pass the blame on to someone else, and whether he demonstrates remorse or not.

2 Once the pleas have been written, volunteers could come and read them out to the class, with the wider group deciding whether or not each one has the desired effect on the audience.

Children should be reminded that the plea is intended to persuade, to ensure that they are writing for this purpose.

Children could focus on events and the cause and consequences of these.

Children should try to be as emotional and persuasive as possible, using various techniques to sway the reader.

Main activity 8

The Drum sequel

AFTER READING
THE DRUM

- **Children should be able to:**

 in narratives, describe settings, characters and atmosphere and integrate dialogue to convey character and advance the action; select appropriate grammar and vocabulary.

 link ideas across paragraphs using a wider range of cohesive devices.

 draw inferences such as inferring characters' feelings, thoughts and motives from their actions, and justify inferences with evidence; predict what might happen from details stated and implied.

1 Explain that children are going to write a sequel to *The Drum*. It will be about Tortoise discovering a third drum with a different magical property.

2 Children write a short plan for their story. This could take the form of a list of key plot points or a mind map of key phrases.

3 Children write their sequel, replicating the style, tone and characters of the original.

T Children could focus on the events: what happened and when.

D Children think specifically about Tortoise and how his character might change or develop based on the consequences in the story.

— **Main activity 9** —

Tortoise's judgement

AFTER READING
THE DRUM

- **Children should be able to:**

 draw inferences such as inferring characters' feelings, thoughts and motives from their actions, and justify inferences with evidence.

 articulate and justify answers, arguments and opinions; give well-structured descriptions, explanations and narratives for different purposes; participate in discussions, presentations, performances, role play, improvisations and debates.

1 Divide the class into groups of four and explain that each group needs to come up with a suitable punishment for Tortoise.

2 Encourage children to think about the effect of Tortoise's actions on the wider community, how much damage he causes, the long-lasting impact, and his motives. They should consider whether a punishment, community service or forgiveness would be the best option.

3 Once the groups have finished, ask each one to explain their judgement to the rest of the class, who should decide whether they agree or not, and why.

4 Encourage a debate between the different groups, supporting children to argue coherently using evidence from the text to support their views.

— **Main activity 10** —

Diary entry

DURING READING

5 x ⏱40

- **Children should be able to:**

  ✏️ identify the audience for and purpose of the writing; select appropriate grammar and vocabulary; use a wide range of devices to build cohesion within and across paragraphs.

  🔤 link ideas across paragraphs using a wider range of cohesive devices; use the semi-colon, colon and dash.

  📖 draw inferences such as inferring characters' feelings, thoughts and motives from their actions, and justify inferences with evidence.

1. Explain that children are going to write diary entries for each of the main characters from the stories listed below.

2. Children should think about how the characters feel during different points of the stories, what they learn about themselves and how they change through the course of the story.
   - *The Drum* (p 29–60): Tortoise
   - *A Lion Hunt* (p 61–71): the narrator
   - *Sosu's Call* (p 73–82): Sosu
   - *The Little Blue Boy* (p 83–92): Little Blue Boy
   - *Citronella* (p 123–128): Citronella

   🇹 Children could focus on the events: what happened and when.

   🇩 Children could focus on the emotional impact of what happens to the characters.

Main activities 11–15

Newspaper report

AFTER READING
THE LITTLE BLUE BOY

3 × **45** **Resources required:** a variety of newspaper articles from different papers (if possible, coverage of the same event from different newspapers)

- **Children should be able to:**

 identify the audience for and purpose of the writing; select appropriate grammar and vocabulary; use a wide range of devices to build cohesion within and across paragraphs; use further organisational and presentational devices to structure text and to guide the reader; assess the effectiveness of their own and others' writing.

 link ideas across paragraphs using a wider range of cohesive devices.

 identify and discuss themes and conventions in and across a wide range of writing; discuss and evaluate how authors use language … considering the impact on the reader.

1. Explain that children are going to look at some newspaper reports and then write news articles of their own.

2. **In the first session,** divide the class into groups of four and hand out a couple of articles to each group – ideally on the same story – explaining that groups should read the articles and discuss the way in which the different newspapers have approached and presented the same story. Encourage children to think about bias, angle, emotive appeal, headlines, dramatic effect, the level of information, accuracy, etc.

3. **In the second session,** children write an article about the birth of Little Blue Boy. This should be based on the story *The Little Blue Boy* and look at the impact of his arrival on his family and the wider community.

4. **In the third session,** children should write a report about a futuristic scenario, based on changes that are happening in the world around them. This could be a look at climate change, deforestation, population growth, politics, etc. Children could use *Half a Day* for inspiration.

5. Encourage children to think about the angle they take, how they want to influence their reader, whether to include quotes or statements and what images would support their reports.

6. Children should also include a headline and tagline.

7. Once the articles are finished, you could hand them out around the class so that children read each other's work. They can comment on the impact the reports had on them, whether their opinion was swayed and how informative they found them.

This activity works well with Starter activity 18.

Main activities 16–18

Lagos

AFTER READING
BULUBULU AND BAMBOKO

2 x ⏱45 **Resources required:** globe or atlases, information books or access to the internet, recording equipment (optional)

- **Children should be able to:**

  ✏️ identify the audience for and purpose of the writing; note and develop initial ideas, drawing on reading and research where necessary.

  💬 articulate and justify answers, arguments and opinions; give well-structured descriptions, explanations and narratives for different purposes; participate in discussions, presentations, performances, role play, improvisations and debates; understand the difference between vocabulary typical of informal speech and vocabulary appropriate for formal speech and writing.

  🌐 use maps, atlases, globes and digital / computer mapping to locate countries and describe features studied.

  📄 retrieve, record and present information from non-fiction.

1. Explain that children are going to work in groups to develop travel documentaries about Lagos, Nigeria.

2. **In the first session,** divide the class into groups of four. The documentaries should have a specific focus, e.g. 'Have an adventure in Lagos', 'Little-known Lagos', 'Luxurious Lagos', 'Lagos for backpackers'. Ask groups to decide on a topic to focus on, or allocate them accordingly.

3. Ask children to locate Lagos on a globe or atlas. Then ask them to research Lagos and make notes about what they'd like to include in their travel documentary, e.g. places to visit, climate, historical context, places to stay, national holidays or festivals of interest.

4. Children choose who in the group will present on which element of the documentary. Then they start to write the material for the documentary. Remind them to think about their audience and whether they are going to use a formal or informal tone.

5. **In the second session,** groups finish off writing their material and then film their documentaries. Encourage children to think about music and images to include. If you don't have recording equipment, they could just perform their documentaries.

6. Once all the documentaries have been created, you could watch them together, or show them in an assembly or to a wider group.

Main activities 19–20

My dream home

AFTER READING: BULUBULU AND BAMBOKO

Resources required: paper, pencils

- **Children should be able to:**

 use research and develop design criteria to inform the design of innovative, functional, appealing products that are fit for purpose, aimed at particular individuals or groups.

 improve their mastery of art and design techniques, including drawing, painting and sculpture with a range of materials.

 identify the audience for and purpose of the writing; select appropriate grammar and vocabulary.

 articulate and justify answers, arguments and opinions; participate in discussions, presentations, performances, role play, improvisations and debates.

1. Explain to the children that they're going to design their own dream houses.

2. Ask children to start the design work of their house by thinking about how big they want it to be, who's going to live there and how the space will be used. They should also think about the space around the house: land, gardens, balconies, decking, swimming pool, etc.

3. Children start the first stage of the design work: creating rough sketches and drawings to show how they'd like their house to look. Encourage children to be experimental and adventurous, to do some research into other extraordinary buildings and to think outside the box.

4. When they are happy, children can create a final drawing. It should include clear labels and lots of detail.

5. When the designs are complete, children accompany their drawings with a short description and explanation of their dream house, covering the reasons for designing it as they have, any specific features, what makes it stand out and who would benefit from living in it.

6. Invite children to come up and present their dream homes to the rest of the group.

This activity may run over into another session. Children could add in drawings of the interior features of their dream house, such as kitchens, bathrooms and even furniture.

Main activity 21

A day in the life

AFTER READING
MISS JOHNSON

 Resources required: examples of some 'day in the life' stories from the internet (e.g. paramedic, police officer, archaeologist, author)

- **Children should be able to:**

 identify the audience for and purpose of the writing; select appropriate grammar and vocabulary; use a wide range of devices to build cohesion within and across paragraphs.

 link ideas across paragraphs using a wider range of cohesive devices.

 identify and discuss themes and conventions in and across a wide range of writing; discuss and evaluate how authors use language ... considering the impact on the reader.

1. Children are going to write about a day in their lives, inspired by *Miss Johnson*.
2. Hand out some examples of the 'day in the life' articles that you have found online, and look at them together, or in small groups.
3. Ask children for feedback on how much they found out about the person, how the information about their life was presented and the level of detail provided. Ask them about the style of writing, whether it was formal or informal, and how it made them feel as readers.
4. Ask children to write their own 'day in the life', which should reflect what an average day in their life is like: what they do, what they eat, who they see and how their routine makes them feel, e.g. the aspects that they enjoy or dread.

T Children storyboard their 'day in the life'.

S Children focus on concrete ideas such as the events themselves.

D Children explain why they do the things they do, or why they enjoy some things but not others, providing more insight into their personality and character.

Main activity 22

A story with no sense

AFTER READING
CITRONELLA

- **Children should be able to:**

  identify the audience for and purpose of the writing; select appropriate grammar and vocabulary; use a wide range of devices to build cohesion within and across paragraphs.

  link ideas across paragraphs using a wider range of cohesive devices; use the semi-colon, colon and dash.

1 Children are going to write a story focusing on one of the senses, or more precisely on life *without* one of the senses. They can choose for their character to have no sense of smell or taste, or to be blind or deaf.

2 Explain that children's stories can be about anything: they don't have to be related to *Citronella*. Encourage them to think about how they can set the scene and introduce their character, what other sense they might rely on and how it might feel to have the disability that they do. Or perhaps it doesn't feel like a disability at all?

As an alternative to a narrative, this could be written as a memoir or autobiography, diary entry or letter.

Main activity 23

A portrait

AFTER READING
FATHER, WHO ARE YOU?

Resources required: art materials to create a drawing, painting, collage or sculpture

- **Children should be able to:**

  improve their mastery of art and design techniques, including drawing, painting and sculpture with a range of materials.

1 Explain to the class that they're going to create a portrait or 3D model of someone important to them, inspired by *Father, Who Are You?*

2 The piece can be a drawing, painting, collage or sculpture, which captures what that person means to them.

3 Explain to children that they can create their impressions from memory or from a photograph.

4 Once they've finished, children could present their pieces to the rest of the class, explaining who they've created and what that person means to them.

This activity may run over more than one session.

Main activity 24

Story with a message

AFTER READING

- **Children should be able to:**

 identify the audience for and purpose of the writing; select appropriate grammar and vocabulary; in narratives, describe settings, characters and atmosphere and integrate dialogue to convey character and advance the action; use a wide range of devices to build cohesion within and across paragraphs.

 link ideas across paragraphs using a wider range of cohesive devices.

1. Once you've finished all the stories in *Chasing the Sun*, talk about how lots of them have a message or a moral.

2. Encourage children to volunteer which story they found the most powerful, and which message had the greatest impact on them, and why.

3. Explain that children are going to be writing their own short story, which contains a message or moral that is important to them.

4. The message can be anything from being kind to others, to helping those less fortunate than yourself, to a message about characteristics like greed, power, honesty, dishonesty, or something much closer to home such as the importance of doing homework or helping out at home.

5. Children should give their stories a title.

T Children work in groups to come up with a plot idea and then each child writes a section of the story, which can then be compiled with the rest.

D Children focus on how to make the message or moral more subtle, so that readers have to dig a little deeper to discover it.

This activity works well with Starter activity 26.

Main activity 25

Animal fable

AFTER READING

 Resources required: examples of animal fables, e.g. Aesop's

- **Children should be able to:**

 identify the audience for and purpose of the writing; select appropriate grammar and vocabulary; in narratives, describe settings, characters and atmosphere and integrate dialogue to convey character and advance the action; use a wide range of devices to build cohesion within and across paragraphs.

 link ideas across paragraphs using a wider range of cohesive devices.

 increase their familiarity with a wide range of books, including … books from other cultures and traditions.

1 Talk about how lots of the stories in *Chasing the Sun* are about animals rather than people and how the animals are often personified and can talk and think like humans.

2 You could look at some other animal fables, e.g. 'The Fox and the Stork', 'The Hare and the Tortoise', or recap any well-known ones as a class.

3 Explain that children are going to write their own animal fable – a short story with animal characters who take on human characteristics.

4 Encourage children to think about how certain animals might behave, what characteristics they have that could be exaggerated in the story, e.g. dogs are often represented as being loyal, monkeys – clever, foxes – sly.

5 Children should give their stories a title.

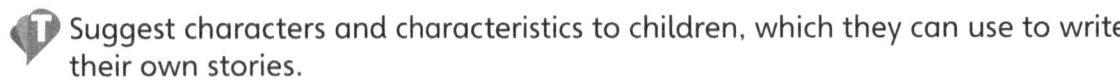 Suggest characters and characteristics to children, which they can use to write their own stories.

Main activity 26

Poetry: animal poems

AFTER READING

4 x 50 **Resources required:** photocopy masters (PCM) 8–10
Children might like to use some of the onomatopoeic words they created in Starter activity 24.

- **Children should be able to:**

 identify the audience for and purpose of the writing; select appropriate grammar and vocabulary.

 prepare poems and plays to read aloud and to perform.

1 Read the poems on PCMs 8–10. You could look at one together or differentiate as shown below.

2 Ask the class what impressions the poems give of the animals they're about, whether they're serious or funny, how they use rhythm and rhyme, whether they provide a powerful image of the animal for the reader, etc.

3 Over four sessions, children are going to write some poems of their own from the perspective of key animal characters from the stories they've read.
   - *Leuk-the-Hare Discovers Man* (p 19–24): Leuk-the-Hare
   - *Why the Mosquito Lives in the Bush* (p 25–28): Iguana
   - *The Drum* (p 29–59): Tortoise
   - *Bulubulu and Bamboko* (p 101–113): a rat

   Remind children that they can include some of the onomatopoeic words from Starter activity 24.

4 Once children have finished their poems, encourage volunteers to read them out to the rest of the class.

T Children use *Poor Crow!* from PCM 8 to support and inspire their writing.

S Children use *To a Fish* from PCM 9 to support and inspire their writing.

D Children use *The Tyger* from PCM 10 to support and inspire their writing.

You may wish to display the class's poems around the classroom.

Main activities 27–30

Plenary activities

Quiz time

BEFORE READING

⏱ 15 **Resources required:** children's quizzes from Main activity 1 *or* your own true or false quiz for the class; timer

- **Children should be able to:**

💬 listen and respond appropriately to adults and their peers; articulate and justify answers, arguments and opinions; use spoken language to develop understanding through speculating, hypothesising, imagining and exploring ideas.

🌍 describe and understand key aspects of physical geography and human geography

1. If children didn't complete Main activity 1, create a true or false quiz, with 20 statements, that introduces them to the topic of Africa. You could include questions about history, geography, culture and nature.

2. Divide the class into pairs and hand out the quizzes. If you're using the children's quizzes, make sure that they don't get their own!

3. Explain that children need to tick 'true' or 'false' for each of the 20 statements in a ten-minute time limit.

4. Set a timer for ten minutes.

5. Once the time is up, return each quiz to the original authors, or get partners to swap, and ask children to mark the quizzes.

6. Encourage children to reflect on the most surprising fact that they learnt.

Plenary activity 1

Animal adjectives

BEFORE READING — SUN, WIND AND CLOUD

⏱ 20   Vocabulary builder **Resources required:** photocopy master (PCM) 3, scissors, stopwatch (optional)

- **Children should be able to:**

   identify how language, structure and presentation contribute to meaning; discuss and evaluate how authors use language, including figurative language, considering the impact on the reader.

  ✏ select appropriate grammar and vocabulary, understanding how such choices can change and enhance meaning.

1 Divide the class into groups of four and give each group a copy of PCM 3. Ask children to cut out the cards.

2 Explain that many of the animals in *Sun, Wind and Cloud* are written about using adjectives that describe the way that they look or sound and adjectives that describe their nature or character.

3 Ask the groups to match each animal with the adjectives that best describe them, placing the physical adjective first and the character adjective second, e.g. 'old, wise tortoise'.

4 Once groups have finished, they could come up with their own examples, e.g. 'yappy, excitable puppy'; 'purring, lazy cat'. Remind them to use traits that are typical of the animals that they're describing, so that the answer will be clear.

5 Groups can create their own word cards (they could turn over the cards from PCM 3 and write on the back of them), mix them up and swap them with another group to see whether they can complete 'Animal adjectives' correctly. Timing groups to do this could bring in a competitive element.

Plenary activity 2

Freeze frame

BEFORE READING — LEUK-THE-HARE DISCOVERS MAN

⏱ 15

- **Children should be able to:**

   participate in discussions, presentations, performances, role play, improvisations and debates.

   explain and discuss their understanding of what they have read; provide reasoned justifications for their views.

1 Once you've read *Leuk-the-Hare Discovers Man*, ask children to recap the central message of the story, including how the message is conveyed.

2 Divide the class into pairs and ask each pair to create a freeze frame of a moment from the story which they think best conveys the message.

3 Ask children to explain why they chose the scene they did.

Plenary activity 3

37

Leuk's revenge

**AFTER READING
LEUK-THE-HARE
DISCOVERS MAN**

(15) **Resources required:** paper, coloured pencils

- **Children should be able to:**

 identify the audience for and purpose of the writing; select appropriate grammar and vocabulary, understanding how such choices can change and enhance meaning.

 link ideas across paragraphs using a wider range of cohesive devices.

 draw inferences such as inferring characters' feelings, thoughts and motives from their actions, and justify inferences with evidence.

 participate in discussions, presentations, performances, role play, improvisations and debates.

1. Ask children to imagine how Leuk-the-Hare's feelings changed throughout the story. How did he feel when he was locked in the cubby hole? How about when the child pulled him out? Or when the dogs were released to chase him?

2. Ask children what they think Leuk's impression of Man is. Was Diargogne-the-spider correct about Man being a 'dangerous animal'?

3. Divide the class into pairs. Ask each pair to come up with an act of revenge that Leuk-the-Hare could enact on Man in response to the way he's treated.

4. Encourage children to think about something that is cunning and will teach Man a valuable lesson, rather than just being aggressive or cruel.

(T) Children draw a picture of their act of revenge.

(S) Children use role play to present their act of revenge.

(D) Children write the act of revenge as a sequel or alternative ending. Remind them to use the same style and tone as the author.

Plenary activity 4

Vocabulary quiz

DURING READING

4 x  Vocabulary builder **Resources required:** photocopy masters (PCM) 4–7

- **Children should be able to:**

 use relevant strategies to build their vocabulary.

1. At four points during reading, explain that the class is going to play a quiz, using vocabulary from the stories. It can be played as a class or in pairs.
2. Photocopy the following.
   - PCM 4 (for quiz 1 after pages 9–24)
   - PCM 6 (for quiz 3 after pages 101–113)
   - PCM 5 (for quiz 2 after pages 61–71)
   - PCM 7 (for quiz 4 after pages 115–121)
3. As you read each question, children need to work out the word that is described.

Write the answers, or first letters of them, on the board in a random order, so that children just have to match the correct word to the definition.

Plenary activities 5–8

Find a resolution

AFTER READING
WHY THE MOSQUITO LIVES IN THE BUSH

- **Children should be able to:**

 identify the audience for and purpose of the writing; select appropriate grammar and vocabulary, understanding how such choices can change and enhance meaning.

 link ideas across paragraphs using a wider range of cohesive devices.

 participate in discussions, presentations, performances, role play, improvisations and debates.

1. Divide the class into pairs. Explain that each pair needs to think about a point in the story at which an alternative course of action could have dramatically altered the end result of the death of the baby owl. Examples of points in the plot include:
   - the Iguana puts sticks in his ears
   - the Rabbit scampers about in daylight
   - the Boa constrictor goes to hide in the rabbit hole
   - the Crow panics and raises an alarm
   - the Monkey jumps about in the trees.
2. Pairs should decide on the alternative version of events, the characters involved and the way the original story will change, then storyboard or write new versions.
3. Once the new versions are finished, invite pairs to share theirs with the class, either reading them out, summarising them or acting them out.

 Children could think more about how the characters feel, and the impact of events on them emotionally.

Plenary activity 9

39

Word discovery

DURING READING

2 x Vocabulary builder **Resources required:** dictionaries

- **Children should be able to:**

   select appropriate grammar and vocabulary, understanding how such choices can change and enhance meaning.

  use dictionaries to check the spelling and meaning of words.

  use relevant strategies to build their vocabulary.

1 Before reading *The Drum* and *A Lion Hunt*, explain that children need to look out for any new or unusual words or phrases that they come across in the stories, and list them.

2 Once you've finished each story, ask children to use a dictionary to look up any words that they didn't understand. Then children can choose one of the words and write a sentence of their own using it.

3 Encourage children to share their sentences with a partner or the whole class.

D Children could try using the same word in different contexts.

Plenary activities 10–11

The drums

AFTER READING
SOSU'S CALL

 Resources required: drums, or items that can be used as drums (e.g. pots and pans, boxes, tins)

- **Children should be able to:**

  listen and respond appropriately to adults and their peers; participate in discussions, presentations, performances, role play, improvisations and debates.

   play and perform in solo and ensemble contexts, using their voices and playing musical instruments with increasing accuracy, fluency, control and expression; improvise and compose music for a range of purposes.

1 Divide the class into groups of four. Explain that each group needs to come up with a piece of music using the drums. Children can use other sound effects or vocals to support their pieces of music.

2 Encourage each group to come up with something original and inspired by *Sosu's Call* and the use of the drums in it.

3 Once groups have had a chance to compose and practise a short piece, they should perform it to the class.

4 Encourage the rest of the class to feed back to the musicians on what they thought of it, how it made them feel and whether they felt it was suitably linked to the story.

D Children could write a short blurb explaining their piece of music, its origins and what it represents.

Plenary activity 12

An artist's impression

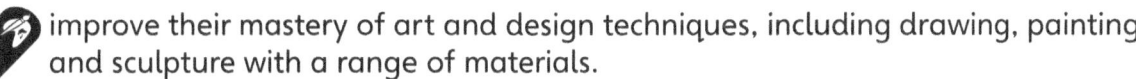

AFTER READING
HALF A DAY

 Resources required: paper, paints or coloured pencils, modelling materials

- **Children should be able to:**

  improve their mastery of art and design techniques, including drawing, painting and sculpture with a range of materials.

  identify the audience for and purpose of the writing; select appropriate grammar and vocabulary, understanding how such choices can change and enhance meaning.

  listen and respond appropriately to adults and their peers; articulate and justify answers, arguments and opinions.

  prepare poems and plays to read aloud and to perform, showing understanding through intonation, tone and volume so that the meaning is clear to an audience.

1 Explain to the class that they are going to create an artists' impression of either the way the world looked to the narrator before he went to school, or the way it looked to him when he was walking home.

2 Encourage children to think about how to represent the change in atmosphere, as well as the physical changes. They can create an image through art or sculpture or by writing a poem.

3 Encourage children to think carefully about how the narrator feels about the environment, and how they can represent this through their piece of work.

4 Once everyone's finished, encourage children to share their artistic impressions.

Plenary activity 13

All change

AFTER READING
HALF A DAY

 Resources required: paper, paints or coloured pencils

- **Children should be able to:**

   identify the audience for and purpose of the writing; select appropriate grammar and vocabulary, understanding how such choices can change and enhance meaning.

   link ideas across paragraphs using a wider range of cohesive devices.

   improve their mastery of art and design techniques, including drawing, painting and sculpture with a range of materials.

   articulate and justify answers, arguments and opinions; give well-structured descriptions, explanations and narratives for different purposes, including for expressing feelings.

   prepare poems and plays to read aloud and to perform, showing understanding through intonation, tone and volume so that the meaning is clear to an audience.

1 Explain that children will describe something that's changed in their community or neighbourhood from the time they started school. They could do this as a piece of prose, a poem or a piece of art. Some examples might include: more housing, fewer parks or green spaces, fewer small local shops, more homeless people. These ideas could be displayed to inspire ideas, or a brief discussion with the class could get the children thinking of their own ideas.

2 Once everyone's finished, encourage children to share their pieces of work.

T Children focus on the physical description of the change that's happened to their community or neighbourhood.

D Children focus on how the change has affected them and others.

Plenary activity 14

Rat habitat

⏱ 15

**BEFORE READING
BULUBULU AND BAMBOKO**

- **Children should be able to:**
  - identify the audience for and purpose of the writing; select appropriate grammar and vocabulary, understanding how such choices can change and enhance meaning.
  - use research and develop design criteria to inform the design of innovative, functional, appealing products that are fit for purpose; evaluate their ideas and products.
  - articulate and justify answers, arguments and opinions; participate in discussions, presentations, performances, role play, improvisations and debates.
  - improve their mastery of art and design techniques, including drawing.
  - identify how animals and plants are adapted to suit their environment in different ways and that adaptation may lead to evolution.

1 Divide the class into pairs and explain that each pair is going to design a habitat for a rat. If the class have completed Starter activity 19, the habitat can be based on the information they have gathered. Otherwise, it can be based on their existing knowledge and some assumptions.

2 The habitats should represent what would best provide for a rat's needs and take all their character traits into account:
   - what they eat and drink
   - how much exercise they do
   - whether they need to be warm or cold
   - how they co-habit with each other.

3 Children draw their habitat, including any important features and list the materials and supplies they would need to construct it.

4 Once pairs have finished, they could write a short piece explaining and justifying their decisions, and / or present it to the rest of the class.

It is preferable to have completed Starter activity 19 before doing this.

Plenary activity 15

Pros and cons

AFTER READING
BULUBULU AND BAMBOKO

- **Children should be able to:**

  select appropriate grammar and vocabulary, understanding how such choices can change and enhance meaning.

  articulate and justify answers, arguments and opinions; participate in discussions, presentations, performances, role play, improvisations and debates.

  identify how animals and plants are adapted to suit their environment in different ways and that adaptation may lead to evolution.

1 Divide the class into pairs. Ask each pair to write a pros and cons list about the two rat habitats: Victoria Island and Mushin. Pairs could work together to create both pros and cons lists, or they could tackle one habitat each.

2 Encourage children to think beyond the physical appearance of the habitats to the impact that the environment has on the rats.

3 When they have finished, pairs discuss their lists and decide which habitat they feel is more appropriate.

4 Encourage the class to come back together to discuss which habitat is the best.

Plenary activity 16

Predict the future

AFTER READING
BULUBULU AND BAMBOKO

- **Children should be able to:**

  identify the audience for and purpose of the writing; select appropriate grammar and vocabulary, understanding how such choices can change and enhance meaning.

  articulate and justify answers, arguments and opinions; use spoken language to develop understanding through speculating, hypothesising, imagining and exploring ideas; participate in discussions, presentations, performances, role play, improvisations and debates.

  predict what might happen from details stated and implied.

1 Ask children to think about the different lives that the two rats have had, based on where they live.

2 Recap the decisions that Bulubulu and Bamboko make at the end (Bulubulu staying in Victoria Island to have a family, and Bamboko returning to Mushin).

3 Divide the class into pairs and ask children to discuss what might happen to both rat families next.

4 Children can storyboard their predictions, or write notes, one or two opening paragraphs or a summary. Alternatively, they could act out their predictions.

You could extend this activity by asking children to start writing a sequel to Bulubulu and Bamboko.

Plenary activity 17

What's next, Miss Johnson?

AFTER READING
MISS JOHNSON

- **Children should be able to:**

   articulate and justify answers, arguments and opinions; use spoken language to develop understanding through speculating, hypothesising, imagining and exploring ideas; listen and respond appropriately to adults and their peers.

   draw inferences such as inferring characters' feelings, thoughts and motives from their actions, and justify inferences with evidence; predict what might happen from details stated and implied.

1 Re-read the last paragraph of *Miss Johnson*.

2 Divide the class into pairs and ask everyone to come up with some ideas about what Miss Johnson might do next. Encourage them to be as creative and imaginative as possible, and to use what they already know about her, including how she felt about her job and how the art changed her.

3 Once they have had five minutes, encourage each pair to share their ideas with the class.

4 Encourage children to debate which scenario is most and least plausible, and why.

D Children could write up Miss Johnson's next steps as a sequel.

Plenary activity 18

Antonyms

AFTER READING
MISS JOHNSON

 Vocabulary builder

- **Children should be able to:**

   discuss and evaluate how authors use language, including figurative language; explore the meaning of words in context.

  use relevant strategies to build their vocabulary.

   understand how words are related by meaning as synonyms and antonyms.

1 Discuss how the author of *Miss Johnson* uses language, in particular how the words she uses to describe Miss Johnson's work are very different from the words she uses to describe the impact that art has on her.

2 Ask children to find examples of words that describe how Miss Johnson is feeling. They should sort these words into two columns, headed 'work' and 'art'.

3 Explain, if necessary, that opposite words are called antonyms. If it's helpful, you could display some, e.g. courage, cowardice; miserable, cheerful; dismal, bright.

4 Ask children to find two sets of antonyms by comparing the two columns (e.g. they could have 'bored' and 'excited / fascinated / dazzled'; 'morose' and 'overjoyed').

5 Bring the class back together and discuss children's answers.

This activity works well after completing Plenary activity 8.

Plenary activity 19

Describing words

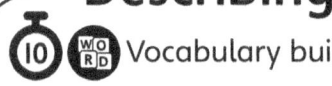

 Vocabulary builder

AFTER READING
MISS JOHNSON

- **Children should be able to:**

  use relevant strategies to build their vocabulary; listen and respond appropriately to adults and their peers; articulate and justify answers, arguments and opinions.

1 Ask children to think about two things in their lives that they feel very differently about, e.g. sport and art, eating dinner at home and at a restaurant, being outdoors and indoors, seeing friends and being alone.

2 Ask children to create two columns, each one headed with the name of what they're describing, and then to list as many words as they can that each activity conjures up.

3 Encourage children to think of words that will have a high impact on their reader, that capture what the activity means to them, and that tell the reader as much as possible.

4 Once children are finished, invite volunteers to call out the words that they think have the most 'wow factor' and then to explain which activity they describe.

This activity will be more effective after completing Plenary activity 19.

Plenary activity 20

Soundscape

AFTER READING
CITRONELLA

2 x  **Resources required:** recording equipment (optional), instruments and other items that will make sounds

- **Children should be able to:**

   articulate and justify answers, arguments and opinions; give well-structured descriptions, explanations and narratives for different purposes; listen and respond appropriately to adults and their peers.

   listen with attention to detail and recall sounds.

1 Divide the class into groups of five. Explain that each group will be creating a soundscape: a recording of an identifiable sound that represents or means something to them. The groups will play their soundscapes to the rest of the class, who will have to guess what the sound is and what it represents.

2 **In the first session,** ask the groups to create their soundscapes using the recording equipment. The soundscape only needs to be 30 seconds long, but it must be clear and recognisable. It can be of anything, from rain falling to birdsong to children in the playground. Once they've recorded it, the group should prepare a short explanation about why they chose their soundscape.

3 **In the second session,** ask the groups to play their soundscapes to the rest of the class, who have to guess what the sounds are and what each soundscape represents. Then the creators of the soundscape justify and explain their choice.

If you don't have access to recording equipment, children could turn their backs while a group performs, so that they cannot see the instruments / items used.

Plenary activities 21–22

Sequence of emotions

AFTER READING
FATHER, WHO ARE YOU?

 Resources required: paper, coloured pencils

- **Children should be able to:**

  draw inferences such as inferring characters' feelings, thoughts and motives from their actions, and justify inferences with evidence.

1. Divide the class into pairs.

2. Display the following emotions, which Boniswa experiences. Write them in this order, but without the numbers in brackets (which show the correct order).

   - soothed (9)
   - afraid (5)
   - proud (10)
   - frightened (1)
   - sad (2)
   - unconfident (4)
   - happy (7)
   - shy (6)
   - nervous (3)
   - sad (8)

3. Ask each pair to put the emotions into the right order to reflect the 'journey' that Boniswa goes on. Some of the emotions are directly referenced in the text, and some will require children to infer Boniswa's feelings.

4. Once children have done this correctly, explain that they're going to create a pictorial representation of the emotional journey. This could be a line graph or timeline, with the different emotions represented in some way, e.g. through colour, images or numbers.

You could display the emotional charts around the classroom.

Plenary activity 23

Musical themes

AFTER READING

Resources required: recording equipment, musical instruments, access to the internet or music streaming service

- **Children should be able to:**

  articulate and justify answers, arguments and opinions; give well-structured descriptions, explanations and narratives for different purposes; listen and respond appropriately to adults and their peers.

  appreciate and understand a wide range of high-quality live and recorded music drawn from different traditions and from great composers and musicians; play and perform in solo and ensemble contexts, using their voices and playing musical instruments with increasing accuracy, fluency, control and expression; improvise and compose music for a range of purposes.

1. Divide the class into pairs. Each pair needs to choose a musical theme for every story: a soundtrack for the book.

2. Encourage children to think about what sort of music would complement each story, e.g. something with or without words, relaxing and calm or lively and dramatic, fast or slow.

3. Explain that pairs can choose music they already know, compose their own music, hum or sing, or just make a note of what they have in mind, e.g. 'something with a slow, heavy beat'.

4. Once pairs have finished, encourage volunteers to present their soundtrack ideas to the rest of the class.

5. The class should feed back as to the impact of the proposed soundtracks.

   Children could do this for a story or two, rather than the whole collection.

   Children could write a short summary about why each piece of music is well suited to that particular story.

Plenary activity 24

An animation

AFTER READING

- **Children should be able to:**

 give well-structured descriptions, explanations and narratives for different purposes; participate in discussions, presentations, performances, role play, improvisations and debates; articulate and justify answers, arguments and opinions; consider and evaluate different viewpoints, attending to and building on the contributions of others.

 identify the audience for and purpose of the writing; select appropriate grammar and vocabulary.

1. Divide the class into groups of three or four. Explain that children are going to imagine a TV company is interested in making one of the stories from the collection into an animation.

2. Children need to choose the story that they think would work best in this format and then write a pitch for it, explaining why it would work, how it could be adapted and what music and sound effects would enhance it.

3. Once the pitches have been written, ask each group to present their choice to the rest of the class.

4. Once everyone has presented, ask the class to vote on the most compelling pitch, reminding them that they can't vote for their own!

Plenary activity 25

Poetry: performances

AFTER READING

2 × ⏱ **Resources required:** photocopy masters (PCM) 8–10, recording equipment (optional)

- **Children should be able to:**

  📖 prepare poems and plays to read aloud and to perform.

  💬 participate in discussions, presentations, performances, role play, improvisations and debates.

1. Divide the class into groups of two, three or four, and explain that each group will create a performance of one of the poems (PCM 8–10) for the rest of the class.

2. **In the first session,** ask groups to start planning and preparing for their presentations. Explain that they need to think about what role everyone in the group will have, how to clearly get across the message of the poem to the audience and whether they need music or sound effects to enhance their performance. Children need to be able to recite their poems by heart as part of their performance.

3. **In the second session,** children take it in turns to perform their poems to the class.

   ⓣ Children perform *Poor Crow!* from PCM 8.

   ⓢ Children perform *To a Fish* from PCM 9.

   ⓓ Children perform *The Tyger* from PCM 10.

Performances could be recorded or filmed, or presented to a wider audience such as at an assembly or parent evening.

Plenary activity 26–27

Country competition

AFTER READING

 Resources required: photocopy master (PCM) 11, globes / atlases

- **Children should be able to:**
  - use maps, atlases, globes and digital / computer mapping to locate countries and describe features studied.
  - listen and respond appropriately to adults and their peers.

1 The stories from the collection originate from lots of different countries. Display a list of the countries mentioned in 'About the Authors' (pages 139–143): Ghana, Côte d'Ivoire, Kenya, Egypt, Nigeria, South Africa, Senegal, Mauritius.

2 Divide the class into pairs and give each pair PCM 11 and a globe or atlas. Explain that each pair has to locate every country on the list and mark it on the map as quickly as they can. The first pair to find each country in the quickest time will win.

Plenary activity 28

Country fact file

AFTER READING

Resources required: access to the internet, non-fiction books about African countries, globes / atlases

- **Children should be able to:**
  - use maps, atlases, globes and digital / computer mapping to locate countries and describe features studied; describe and understand key aspects of physical geography.
  - identify the audience for and purpose of the writing; select appropriate grammar and vocabulary; use further organisational and presentational devices to structure text and to guide the reader.
  - retrieve, record and present information from non-fiction.

1 Divide the class into groups of two or three and explain that they're going to create a fact file about one of the countries from where the stories originate: Ghana, Côte d'Ivoire, Kenya, Egypt, Nigeria, South Africa, Senegal, Mauritius. Allocate each group a country.

2 Children's fact files should include some basic information about the country: size, geographical location, population, capital city, any particular features or landmarks, terrain, any indigenous species, etc.

3 Remind children to use a variety of devices to structure the text and make it easier for the reader, e.g. bullet points, labels or captions. Ask children to include a picture in their fact file, either drawn or sourced online.

4 Once the fact files are finished, create an Africa fact file for the class library. Children could add to it during other projects or as part of their creative writing classes.

Children could create a fact file for more than one country.

Plenary activity 29

Our country vs ...

AFTER READING

⏱ 15 **Resources required:** access to the internet, non-fiction books about African countries

- **Children should be able to:**

 describe and understand key aspects of physical geography.

 listen and respond appropriately to adults and their peers; articulate and justify answers, arguments and opinions.

 retrieve, record and present information from non-fiction.

1. Divide the class into pairs. Explain that each pair is going to draw up a comparison list to compare your own country with one of the countries from where the stories originate: Ghana, Côte d'Ivoire, Kenya, Egypt, Nigeria, South Africa, Senegal, Mauritius. If necessary, display the names of the countries so that children can see which they can choose from.

2. Ask children to draw a line down the middle of a piece of paper to create two columns. One column should be headed with your country's name and the other the name of their chosen African country.

3. Explain that pairs need to think of as many things as they can that are different about the two regions. Some things to think about are: climate, wildlife, terrain, population, landscape.

4. Once children have finished, they could repeat with a different African country.

Ⓓ Children could think about similarities as well as differences between the countries.

Plenary activity 30

Sequence of events

PCM 1

Number these events in the order in which they happen in *Why the Mosquito Lives in the Bush.*

_____ The Monkey kills the baby owl.

_____ The Boa constrictor hides in the rabbit hole.

_____ The Crow raises the alarm.

_____ The Mosquito tells his yam story.

_____ The Owl refuses to hoot.

_____ The Rabbit runs out of his hole in daylight.

_____ The Iguana puts sticks in his ears.

_____ Daybreak never comes.

Skim the story to look for the characters' names!

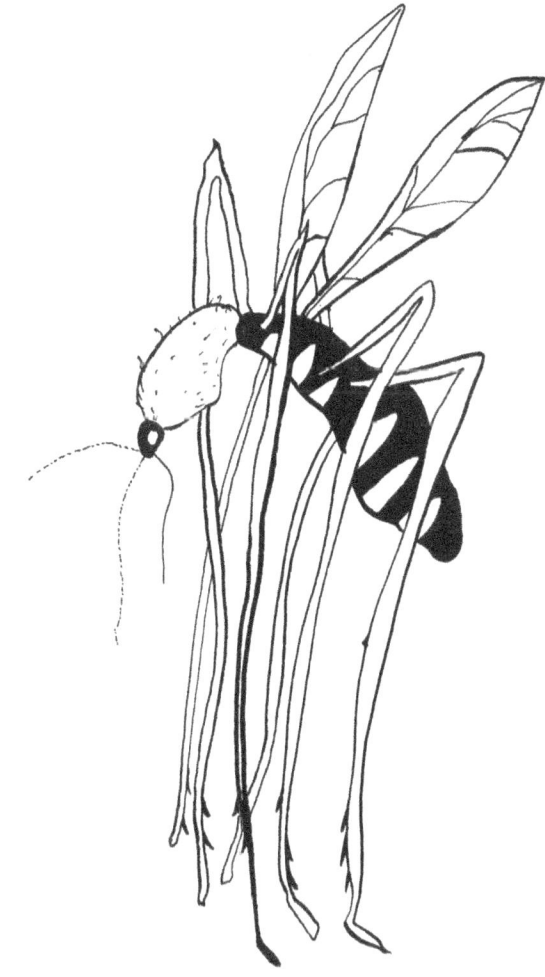

African animals

PCM 2

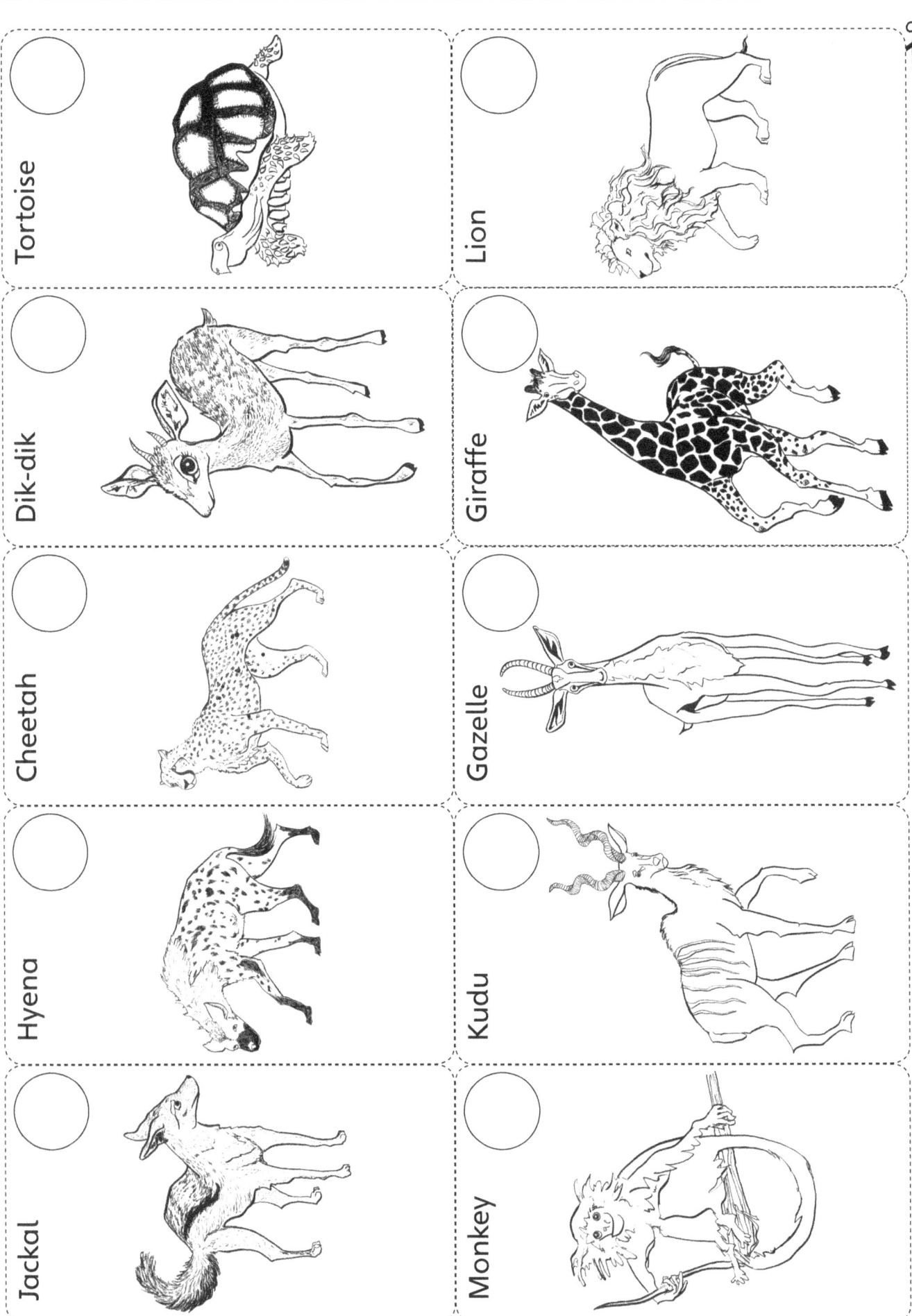

Animal adjectives

PCM 3

tortoise	wise	humble
lion	beautiful	small
crested crane	old	frightening
dik-dik	vain	loud

Vocabulary quiz 1

PCM 4

Use *Leuk-the-Hare Discovers Man* to find the answers to this quiz.

1. What word would you use if someone sees something only partially or briefly? _____

2. What's another word for 'not often' or 'infrequently'? _____

3. Which word means 'group closely together'? _____

4. If something is engraved into another material, what is it? _____

5. What are you doing if you gesture in an exaggerated way to make a point? _____

6. What's the name of something that goes over an animal's mouth to stop it biting? _____

7. What is it called if you search for food or provisions? _____

8. What are you doing if you tease or make fun of someone? _____

9. If someone is being very careful in a dangerous situation, you might say they are 'proceeding with…' _____

10. What is the name of a large, grassy plain, usually found in Africa? _____

11. What's another word for 'brave'? _____

12. What is it to be strong, healthy and full of energy? _____

Vocabulary quiz 2

PCM 5

Use *A Lion Hunt* to find the answers to this quiz.

1. What's a word for being admitted into a group or club, often with a ritual or ceremony? _____

2. If you're communicating with someone, what is that called? _____

3. What's another word for 'boasting'? _____

4. Which word has the same meaning as 'holiday'? _____

5. What word means to move randomly around an area? _____

6. What's the straight line called from the middle to the edge of a circle or sphere? _____

7. What's the word to describe a harsh-sounding noise that comes from the throat? _____

8. If a group of animals suddenly ran together, what would they have done?

   _____

9. If someone is striking fear into someone else, what are they doing?

   _____

10. What's another word for creating interest in something to generate excitement? _____

11. If someone is half asleep or semi-conscious, what state could they be in?

    _____

12. If something moved suddenly and powerfully, what did it do?

    _____

Vocabulary quiz 3

PCM 6

Use *Bulubulu and Bamboko* to find the answers to this quiz.

1. If somewhere is far away from busy, populated areas, what is it?

   _____

2. What is a mixture of harsh, jarring sounds called?_____

3. What is it called if something or someone has a frightening or threatening effect?_____

4. What is another word for 'tease'?_____

5. If you can move easily and nimbly, what are you?_____

6. Which word describes an area of a city where a particular group of people live?_____

7. What would you call something that is very neglected and therefore falling apart?_____

8. What is the name of a refuge or place of safety?_____

9. What is the name for something being passed on to someone else

   _____

10. What is the name for having exclusive possession or control of something?_____

11. What is another word for 'wealthy'?_____

12. What is a large quantity or supply of something called?_____

Vocabulary quiz 4

PCM 7

Use *Miss Johnson* to find the answers to this quiz.

1. What is the name for a loud, unpleasant noise?_____

2. If someone is bad-tempered and miserable, what might they be called?

   _____

3. What is the name given to something that never ends?_____

4. What is another word for 'dullness' or 'repetitiveness'?_____

5. Unknown or unimportant things are said to be in what?_____

6. What is it called when something starts again after a pause

   or interruption?_____

7. Which word means the same as 'confused' or 'bewildered'?_____

8. What is the name for marks or signs that represent something?

   _____

9. What's another way of saying 'come out of and be seen'?

   _____

10. What is it called to make someone accept something?

    _____

11. What do you feel if you are thankful?_____

12. What is the word that means 'moving down'?_____

Poor Crow!

Give me something to eat,
    Good people, I pray;
I have really not had
    One mouthful today!

I am hungry and cold,
    And last night I dreamed
A scarecrow had caught me—
    Good land, how I screamed!

Of one little children
    And six ailing wives
(No, one wife and six children),
    Not one of them thrives.

So pity my case,
    Dear people, I pray;
I'm honest, and really
    I've come a long way.

Mary Mapes Dodge

To a Fish

You strange, astonished-looking, angle-faced,
Dreary-mouthed, gaping wretches of the sea,
Gulping salt-water everlastingly,
Cold-blooded, though with red your blood be graced,
And mute, though dwellers in the roaring waste;
And you, all shapes beside, that fishy be,
Some round, some flat, some long, all devilry,
Legless, unloving, infamously chaste:

O scaly, slippery, wet, swift, staring wights,
What is't ye do? What life lead? eh, dull goggles?
How do ye vary your vile days and nights?
How pass your Sundays? Are ye still but joggles
In ceaseless wash? Still nought but gapes, and bites,
And drinks, and stares, diversified with boggles?

James Henry Leigh Hunt

The Tyger

Tyger Tyger, burning bright,
In the forests of the night;
What immortal hand or eye,
Could frame thy fearful symmetry?

In what distant deeps or skies.
Burnt the fire of thine eyes?
On what wings dare he aspire?
What the hand, dare seize the fire?

And what shoulder, & what art,
Could twist the sinews of thy heart?
And when thy heart began to beat,
What dread hand? & what dread feet?

What the hammer? what the chain,
In what furnace was thy brain?
What the anvil? what dread grasp,
Dare its deadly terrors clasp!

When the stars threw down their spears
And water'd heaven with their tears:
Did he smile his work to see?
Did he who made the Lamb make thee?

Tyger Tyger burning bright,
In the forests of the night:
What immortal hand or eye,
Dare frame thy fearful symmetry?

William Blake

Country competition

PCM 11

Answers

PCM 1: Sequence of events

1. The Mosquito tells his yam story.
2. The Iguana puts sticks in his ears.
3. The Boa constrictor hides in the rabbit hole.
4. The Rabbit runs out of his hole in daylight.
5. The Crow raises the alarm.
6. The Monkey kills the baby owl.
7. The Owl refuses to hoot.
8. Daybreak never comes.

PCM 3: Animal adjectives

old, wise tortoise

loud, frightening lion

beautiful, vain crested crane

small, humble dik-dik

PCM 4: Vocabulary quiz 1

1. glimpses (p19); 2. occasionally (p20); 3. huddle (p20); 4. etched (p21); 5. gesticulating (p21); 6. muzzle (p21); 7. forage (p21); 8. mocking (p23); 9. caution (p23); 10. savannah (p23); 11. courageous (p23); 12. vigorous (p23)

PCM 5: Vocabulary quiz 2

1. initiated (p61); 2. interaction (p61); 3. bragging (p61); 4. vacation (p62); 5. roam (p62); 6. radius (p63); 7. guttural (p65); 8. stampeded; 9. terrorising (p67); 10. hyping (p68); 11. trance (p68); 12. surged (p70)

PCM 6: Vocabulary quiz 3

1. remote (p101); 2. cacophony (p102); 3. intimidating (p102); 4. taunt (p103); 5. agile (p103); 6. ghetto (p103); 7. derelict (p104); 8. sanctuary (p104); 9. inherited (p104); 10. monopoly (p105); 11. affluent (p108); 12. abundance (p108)

PCM 7: Vocabulary quiz 4

1. din (p115); 2. morose (p116); 3. infinity (p116); 4. monotony (p116); 5. obscurity (p117); 6. resumes (p118); 7. perplexed (p118); 8. symbol (p119); 9. emerge (p119); 10. impose (p119); 11. gratitude (p120); 12. descending (p120)

PCM 11: Country competition

Clockwise from top left: Senegal, Nigeria, Egypt, Kenya, Mauritius, South Africa, Ghana, Côte d'Ivoire